JOURNEY TO THE PAST

MEDIEVAL PARIS

Anna Cazzini Tartaglino

and

Nanda Torcellan

RAINTREE STECK-VAUGHN PUBLISHERS

A Harcourt Company

Austin · New York
www.steck-vaughn.com

Published by Raintree Steck-Vaughn, an imprint of Steck-Vaughn Company

Library of Congress Cataloging-in-Publication Data

Tartaglino, Anna Cazzini.
   [Parigi medievale. English]
   Medieval Paris / Anna Cazzini Tartaglino, Nanda Torcellan.
      p. cm. — (Journey to the past)
   Includes index.
   ISBN 0-7398-1956-9
      1. Paris (France)—History—To 1515—Juvenile literature. [1. Paris (France)—History—To 1515. 2. Paris (France)—Social life and customs. 3. France—History—Medieval period, 987–1515. 4. Middle Ages— History.] I. Torcellan, Nanda, 1934– II. Title. III. Series.

DC725 .T37 2001
944'.3602—dc21   00-045697

Translated by: Mary Stuttard
Editorial Director: Cristina Cappa Legora
Editorial Coordinator: Cristina Drago
Editor: Stefano Sibella
Illustrations: Aldo Ripamonti
Graphics: Marco Volpati

Raintree Steck-Vaughn Staff: Marion Corkett, Pam Wells
Project Manager: Lyda Guz
Photo Research: Claudette Landry, Sarah Fraser

Photo Credits:

P.48a ©Superstock; p.49a ©Owen Franken/CORBIS; p.49b ©Michael S. Yamashita/CORBIS; p.48b ©Paul Almasy/CORBIS; p.49c ©Superstock; p.50a ©Robert Holmes/CORBIS; p.50b ©Paul Almasy/CORBIS; p.51a ©Hubert Stadler/CORBIS; p.51b ©Chad Ehlers/International Stock.

All other photographs are from the Archives of IGDA.

Printed and bound in Italy

1 2 3 4 5 6 7 8 9 05 04 03 02 01 00

TABLE OF CONTENTS

All Roads Lead to Paris

In the 13th century, Paris is the first real European capital. Many travelers visit the city, attracted by its monuments, its commerce, and the growing reputation of its university. Most visitors travel by land, but others arrive by sailing along the Seine River. Traveling is not easy, and it's time consuming. It's especially hard during bad weather due to the condition of the roads.

The old Roman roads have been neglected and cannot be used easily. Other roads have stony, bumpy surfaces that become extremely muddy during rain or snow. When the rivers are flooded, bridges are

sometimes destroyed, as occurred with the Grand-Pont, or great bridge, over the Seine in Paris. When this happens, people are forced to ferry across the rivers. Some people, like the pilgrims who visit the holy places spread all across France, journey on foot, others go on horseback or by cart. Along the major routes you can find almshouses or inns where you can rest and eat. Be aware, though, that while you are traveling, you are never really safe from being attacked by bandits or robbed by pickpockets. You will often meet messengers carrying letters written by students from the University of Paris to their families. But the students are the only ones to be so well organized. Anyone else who wishes to send a message can only count on the good will of some kind traveler to deliver it.

Traveling by cart, in good weather, you can cover just over ten leagues per day. On horseback, you can cover fifteen leagues. If you wish to reach Paris by way of the river instead, you can ask for passage on one of the many boats that sail up the Seine from the sea. Or, you might sail on one of the ships loaded with precious goods coming directly from the fairs in the Champagne region. Watch for the women washing clothes on the riverbanks. These washerwomen will be the first people to welcome you to Paris.

- Kiev

yzantium
stantinople)

San Giovanni Acre

Jerusalem

• Damietta
•Mansura

n Sea

Alexandria
(Egypt)

From Paris to...

Distances, in leagues, overland, between Paris and important European cities.

From Marseilles to Paris	200
From Orléans to Paris	32
From Toulouse to Paris	185
From Reims to Paris	35
From Poitiers to Paris	55
From Lyons to Paris	120
From Bourges to Paris	60
From Troyes to Paris	40
From Rome to Paris	400

Distance by sea between France and major ports of call (days at sea in sailing days)

From Marseilles to Tunis	5-6
From Marseilles to Alexandria, Egypt	30
From Marseilles to Ostia, the port of Rome	3

Welcome!

If you approach Paris from the south, you will come across the ancient abbey of Saint-Germain-des-Prés, built in the middle of the meadows. Next, you will see the immense barrier of the city walls and the Saint-Jacques' gate. Once inside the city, you will see the Sainte-Genevieve hill. The Rive Gauche, or Left Bank of the river district, is built around this hill. This neighborhood is sometimes called Outre Petit-Pont, the area beyond the small bridge. It is the seat of various monasteries, colleges, and of the university. Once you take the long, straight road

called Rue Saint-Jacques, shortly you will reach the Petit-Pont, or small bridge, over the Seine. Cross it and you will be on a small island called Ile de la Cité. This is where Paris was born. Here you can admire the cathedral of Notre-Dame, the Palais Royal, King's Palace, Sainte-Chapelle, and Hotel-Dieu. Beyond the island, the city appears to be bursting with houses and churches.

As you leave Ile de la Cité by crossing the Seine over the Grand-Pont, you will sense the bustling activity in the Greve port area and along the wharfs near the church of Saint-Germain-l'Auxerrois. Just a short distance from here, you will find yourself in the Outre Grand-Pont, the area beyond the great bridge, in the Rive Droite, or Right Bank district. This neighborhood is overcrowded and full of life! The streets are crammed with small shops and workshops. Here you will find the famous covered market Les Halles. The two most important streets, Rue Saint-Denis and Rue Saint-Martin, run parallel through the Right Bank as far as the city walls.

The Origins of Paris

In his commentary on the Gallic Wars, Julius Caesar writes of a fortress he calls "Lutetia Parisiorum." This fortress was built by the Parisian Celts, who had established a settlement on an island in the middle of the Seine River. Coins have been found dating back to 100 B.C. that were minted by these people. Caesar records that the Parisian Celts were defeated by one of his lieutenants, Labieno, in 52 B.C. After this defeat, a Roman city developed on the left bank of the Seine around the hill later to be known as Sainte-Genevieve. Because of the city's elevated position, it could be defended. However, Germans and Franks later sacked the city, and its inhabitants were forced to take refuge on the island. They built walls around the island for protection. The city was then named Paris.

1 Seine River
2 Right Bank
3 Left Bank
4 Ile de la Cité
5 Marais
6 Petit-Pont
7 Notre-Dame
8 Hotel-Dieu
9 Palais Royal (King's Palace)
10 Sainte-Chapelle
11 Grand-Pont
12 Place de la Greve
13 Rue Saint-Martin
14 Rue Saint-Denis
15 Halles
16 Saint-Germain-l'Auxerrois
17 Rue Saint-Jacques
18 Sainte-Genevieve
19 Saint-Germain-des-Prés
20 Ile Notre-Dame
21 Ile aux Vaches

Some Useful Information

The most striking thing about Paris is the way it is divided into three separate and very different areas. The city is protected by the imposing walls built by Philip Augustus and is crossed by the Seine River. The island known as Ile de la Cité is situated in the middle of the river. Here is the heart of royal power, the King's Palace, and of religious power, the cathedral of Notre-Dame. To the north lies the Right Bank, called the City. Thanks to its ports and the famous markets, Les Halles, the city is in full economic and commercial expansion.

To the south lies the Left Bank, called the University, because of the schools that have recently developed around the abbey of Sainte-Genevieve. The reputation of these schools is so great that Paris is now considered one of the major cultural centers in Europe. The city is crisscrossed by a tight network of over three hundred streets, lanes, and alleys. Very few of them are paved.

You will be struck by the huge number of religious buildings you see. The Right Bank boasts fourteen parishes; Ile de la Cité, twelve; and the Left Bank, seven. A great deal of land belongs to the religious institutions. The rest belongs to the king, the nobles, and the merchants. Traffic crowds the streets—travelers, monks, students, children, beggars, carts. What noise, bustle and activity!

LOCAL CURRENCY

By the time of the emperor Philip Augustus, the Parisian monetary system had replaced that of all other French cities. The Parisian monetary unit is equal to twenty gross, or sous (both names for old coins). Each sou is in turn worth twelve Parisian deniers. The denier is worth two mailles (pennies). Philip's successor, Louis IX, has had a special gold coin minted called a crown. This coin has the symbol of his royal house struck on one side; a shield bearing the fleur-de-lis, the iris.

But how expensive is it to live in Paris? With one maille (penny), you can buy basic foods like three eggs, a herring, paté (a small meat pie) or a finely ground meats or black-pudding, fruit, and vegetables. Or, you can drink a jug of wine, beer, or cider, or buy half a loaf of bread and some spices. Spices are somewhat more expensive than other foods because they must be shipped to Paris from foreign places. A maille will also buy you a hat, a ring, or a pair of earrings. It will buy sewing articles, like hooks or laces, needles, and thread. For this fee, if you are male, the barbier (barber) will shave you. Or you can watch a show given by acrobats, jugglers, or traveling actors.

WHERE TO FIND FOOD AND LODGING

If travelers who arrive in Paris cannot stay with a friend, they can stay at a guesthouse. Here you can sleep in a simple room and sometimes even find food. Unfortunately guesthouses have the reputation of housing thieves and scoundrels. If you prefer not to stay at a guesthouse, you can seek shelter at a convent. They never turn away travelers. You can eat at an inn. Look carefully, they are sometimes identified by a hanging sign made from straw, wood, or wrought iron. The menu is written out onto a scroll of parchment, which will be shown to you once you sit at a table. You can eat at a tavern, too, but people more often go there to drink. Sometimes, to attract customers, the landlord stands at the door boasting about the excellent quality of his wine. The taverns are lively, noisy places, with people playing at dice. These activities, however, quite often lead to trouble. Fights break out frequently. Taverns are not really fit places for young people.

ADDRESSES AND INTERESTING FACTS

It is not at all difficult to find an address in medieval Paris. Some streets take their names from the places they lead to, like Rue des Champeaux or Rue Saint-Denis. Others take their names from the work carried out on the particular street, like Rue de la Ganterie (the glovemakers' street), Rue des Bouchers (the butchers' street), Rue de la Verrerie (the glassmakers' street), or Rue de la Ferronerie (the ironmongers' street). Or streets may be named after the old owner of the land, like Rue Geoffroy L'Angevin. Or they may be named after the person who built the most impressive residence there, like Rue du Temple. They might also be called after an inn or shop, like Rue de la Colombe (Dove Street), or Rue des Halles (Covered Market Street). They might even be named after a feature of the area, like Rue de l'Arbre-sec (Dry Tree Street), Rue de l'Abreuvoir (Water-Trough Street), or even Rue de l'Egout (Sewer Street).

Street names often indicate neighborhoods where non-French Parisians live. For example, there is a large colony of Bretons living in Paris. These Bretons live along Rue de la Bretonnerie.

DRESS

How Parisians dress shows their wealth and social class. Clerics, craftsmen, workers, and the poor dress simply. They wear long, roughly woven, dull-colored shirts, made of wool or hemp. Their shoes are wooden clogs or open sandals. Merchants wear better quality, more refined clothing. The nobles wear the most luxurious, showy, and stylish clothing. Each garment is made with great care. The material is soft, fine Flemish woolen cloth or Italian silk, dyed in every shade of red, blue, or violet. Often the garments are richly embroidered and are decorated with precious jewels, like rubies, emeralds, and pearls. Women's clothes follow the fashion. At times their dresses have long, trailing trains. At other times, their dresses are tight fitting. The nobles wear shoes made from leather. Wearing a pair of shoes with each shoe a different color is considered very elegant.

In summertime or when traveling, all Parisians wear wide-brimmed hats to protect them from the sun. In winter, they wear hoods to protect themselves from the rain. Different social classes can be recognized by the hats they wear. Each guild of merchants or craftsmen has its own special beret.

WHAT TO DO IN CASE OF ILLNESS

Unfortunately it is easy to fall ill in Paris. The climate varies a great deal. Another major cause of illness is the lack of good hygiene. The houses have no running water or toilets. Piles of trash are left rotting in the streets. Garbage is only occasionally collected. All the waste from the butchers' shops, the markets, and the tanneries is thrown into the streets. The gutters stink, especially when it rains. All of this leads to an increase in the rat and insect population. The water in the Seine River is not pure and often pollutes the wells that provide Paris with its drinking water.

Some illnesses, particularly in children, are caused by spoiled food. It is very difficult to keep food from spoiling, especially in warm weather. Then there are the more serious illnesses like the frequent epidemics of fever and inflammation. These are treated with medicinal poultices and above all with bleeding. The doctor does this believing the blood will "draw out" the illness. If you really need medical treatment, you can ask a druggist or an herbalist, both of whom prepare herbal medicines. If you have a toothache, you need to see the barber. If you want to be treated well and free of charge, go to the Hotel-Dieu (hospital). The number of lepers in Paris has increased greatly since the Crusades. They are treated in isolation, in the leper house called Saint-Lazare or Saint-Ladre, situated outside the city walls.

Although good public hygiene is almost absent, Parisians are keen on personal hygiene. Public baths have existed since Roman times. There are now twenty-six. Streets are often named after the public baths located on them. The public baths are open every day, except Sundays and public holidays. Only the rich have their own bathtubs in their homes.

WHAT CAN YOU EAT IN PARIS?

Bread, meat, and wine make up the Parisians' basic diet. Mealtimes follow the course of the sun and vary according to the season and the social status and income of the family. In general, if they are not invited to a banquet, nobles eat at least two meals a day. They eat dinner in the afternoon, between the third and sixth hour. Supper is eaten after dark, between vespers (evening prayers) and compline (the last prayers of the day). Supper includes soup, boiled meat or fish, and cheese or fruit. Early in the morning, the working classes eat a breakfast of bread and watered-down wine. They have a simple meal during the day, perhaps bread and cheese. Their evening meal is eaten at sunset, after they finish work. At this meal, they eat leek or onion soup.

Chicken is eaten more often than the more expensive meat and game. Parisians prepare a great variety of sauces flavored with spices like pepper, saffron, cinnamon, cloves, and the highly appreciated grain of paradise, or Guinea pepper. Sometimes they use juniper or ginger in their cooking. The Parisians adore anything that tastes bittersweet. So, when flavoring food, they often mix honey (sugar is very rare) with vinegar or with a slightly acid juice that is squeezed from unripe grapes. Food is preserved by using spices or by smoking. During Lent, people eat smoked fish (herring), fish preserved in vinegar, or fresh fish from the Seine or the English Channel. Fish caught in the Channel is carried from Normandy to Paris by a man on horseback, who brings it to the shops and markets in the city.

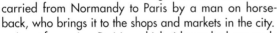

Apart from wine, Parisians drink cider and a beer made from barley and other cereals. Cheeses from the nearby Brie area are very popular. People cook at home over the fireplace. For those who have no chimney, or who have no desire to cook, there are shops that sell cooked food. Peddlers, too, sell ready-made meals. They also sell sweets called oublies, a kind of wafer cone, which are particularly popular. Now, don't you feel hungry?

WHERE CAN YOU SHOP IN PARIS?

Shopping is really easy in Paris, and your choices are enormous. Many shops and markets sell food and as many others sell clothing or household goods. There are special markets, too, like the market of the Halles or the Lendit fair. Other special markets and fairs are held on religious holidays. If you really do not want to tire yourself, you can even shop from home. Sooner or later you will hear the cries of the street peddlers, for the most part women, who sell fresh fish, fruit, and vegetables from the Marais, in addition to, chickens, eggs, and sweets in plenty. And remember to buy candles to light the house. Otherwise you will have only the light from the fireplace, providing, of course, that your house has a fireplace! If you want to read or buy books, you have to go into the neighborhoods of the Left Bank. Because they are close to the university, these areas are full of bookshops. As you see, shopping in Paris is no problem. Just take care not to be swindled!

WEIGHTS AND MEASURES

You will find rather complicated systems of measurement in Paris. The unit of weight is the livre, which is equal to about 12.7 ounces and is divided into 12 portions. Each ounce is equal to a little more than 30 grams. The mark, equal to 8 ounces, is used for weighing precious metals.

Distance is measured in postal leagues, which is the distance between one postal relay station and another, about 2 1/2 miles. The arpent, similar to an acre, is used for measuring area, and equals almost an acre. Length is measured in fathoms, which are roughly equal to 6 1/2 feet. However, the basic unit for measuring length is the Parisian foot, or the King's foot, equal to 14 inches. Fabrics are measured using a rule that is roughly equal to an arm's length. Shorter lengths are measured in thumbs, equal to about 11 inches each, lines, equal to 1 inch, and points, equal to 1/10 inch. To measure the volume of grains, the barrel is used. This is equal to about 144 bushels. Liquids are measured in pints, each equal to about a quart.

MEASURING TIME: HOURS AND CALENDARS

The Parisian calendar is decided by Christian religious festivals. The year begins at Easter, so the first day of the year varies based on the Church calendar. Christmas is one of the principal festivals. People in Paris follow the example of Saint Francis of Assisi in Italy and set up a nativity scene, or creche, in their homes. Epiphany, or the day of the Three Kings, which falls just after Christmas, is an important feast, too. In summer, Parisians celebrate Pentecost, or Whitsuntide. In autumn, they have feast days to remember the saints, All Hallows, and the dead, All Souls. Other days are set aside to honor the patron saints of Paris, Saint Marcel and Saint Genevieve.

The day is divided according to the hours people work, from dawn to sunset. Few people own instruments for measuring time, like sandglasses or hourglasses, or sundials. Mechanical clocks are even more rare. Pierre Pipelard, the goldsmith, built the one you can see in the Sainte-Chapelle. In the city, you can also tell the time by listening to the bells. Every three hours, the bells call the faithful to prayer. The last peal of bells in the day announces the curfew.

CHILDREN IN PARIS

Children in Paris can go to convent primary schools, if their families can afford to pay for them. There they are taught to read and write, to count, and to understand a little Latin. The oldest, most famous school is in the cloister of Notre-Dame. Only the sons of the nobles or the rich go to school, however, because most children are needed to help their parents in their work. But, when they are not helping their parents, many children play in the street. They play games like hopscotch and hide-and-seek. Smaller children enjoy playing with a top, older ones play marbles. Girls play with dolls. In the square and in the fields, you can run around in a rougher game called "soule." In this game, dozens of young men divide into two teams. Then they "fight," with clubs or by using their feet, to gain possession of a ball made either of wood or of skin stuffed with tow (flax or hemp). In winter, when it snows, Parisian children enjoy huge snowball fights. In summer, they race through the streets or swim in the Seine.

THE PARISIANS, WHAT CURIOUS PEOPLE!

Parisians love eating and drinking, as you have probably already realized. The taverns are never empty. Every formal religious festival, like Christmas or Easter, is celebrated with special processions, elaborate meals, and parties in the squares. Each fair, like the Lendit fair or the Saint-Germain-des-Prés fair, each wedding or christening always ends with a banquet. The Parisians love luxury, too. They adore showing off and following or inventing fashions. In fact, to curb his subjects' enthusiasm for fashion, Louis IX has issued a decree obliging them to dress in a more sober and modest way, like good Christians.

The inhabitants of this city have names like Jean, Pierre, Guillaume, Genevieve, Jeanne, and Claudine. Many males are called Charles or Louis, after their kings. Parisians are sociable and talkative. But they do not all greet each other in Latin, like the university students, who exchange the traditional greeting, "Nos fuimus simul in Garlandia," ("We were together in Garlandia," the name of the university neighborhood). They enjoy playing dice games and chess so much that Louis IX has been obliged to make a law against these games. When the weather is good, the Parisians go outside the city walls to the meadows surrounding the abbey of Saint-Germaine-des-Prés. Here, they sing, play, dance in a circle holding hands, or weave garlands and crowns of flowers. They love to watch the shows that the jugglers put on. They also like to watch the miracle plays, performed in the churchyard of Notre-Dame, or the shows and games organized in the many squares.

But the Parisians are hardworking, too. They are organized into powerful craftsmen's métiers (guilds). These groups have gotten so many privileges and powers away from the king that they have been responsible for the birth of a flourishing middle class. Parisians are devoted to their city and to their king. They celebrate the triumphant return of the king from victories over their enemies or from the Crusades.

Notre-Dame

If you cross over to the Ile de la Cité by the Petit-Pont, turn right and walk along to the square where the magnificent new cathedral of Paris, Notre-Dame, stands. You will soon come across a busy building site. Carpenters, bricklayers, stonemasons, blacksmiths, joiners, and glaziers are all working hard under the supervision of foremen from the different guilds. Since 1163, how many years and how much money have been needed to build the cathedral designed by the architects Jean de Chelles and later Pierre de Montreuil! Even if one of the towers is still under construction, the bells already ring out from the other.

There are three doorways decorated with sculptures and dedicated to the Virgin, the Last Judgment, and Saint Anne. Above them are 28 statues of biblical kings. The rose window is a beautiful flower of colored, stained glass. On either side are two huge Gothic windows. Along the sides of the cathedral, where you will find the doorways, one dedicated to Saint Etienne and one to the cloister, you can admire the effect of the flying-buttresses between the huge windows. The brightly painted, stained-glass windows show scenes from the Bible.

Inside, the width and height of the central nave are amazing. On either side, Louis IX has had chapels built to be used for the meetings of the different craftsmen. Religious relics are on display behind the main altar. The silence and the atmosphere created by the colored light filtering through the windows invite you to meditate. Important religious ceremonies are held here. Before leaving for the Crusades, Louis IX came here to pray, and in 1239, he received the relic believed to be the crown of thorns Jesus wore.

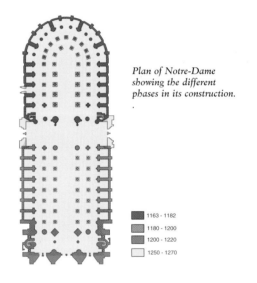

Plan of Notre-Dame showing the different phases in its construction.

■	1163 - 1182
■	1180 - 1200
■	1200 - 1220
□	1250 - 1270

Ring Giving Right of Sanctuary

A large, iron ring is fixed to the doors for whoever seeks help or refuge at night, even criminals. You only have to grasp the ring in order to receive help and protection.

NOTRE-DAME SCHOOL

Notre-Dame School, in the cloisters of the cathedral, is a school for religious orders that also gives lodging and free education to children willing to devote themselves to singing. The Notre-Dame School is also a group of musicians and singers who, at the end of 1100, founded the French school of polyphonic music, music played on an organ with 200 pipes.

The Gargoyles

These are roof waterspouts in the shape of threatening monsters or dragons. They collect rainwater from the roof gutters and spray it down to the ground away from the walls, almost as if they would like to spit away all the evil and vices which threaten men and women.

The Royal Palace

At the eastern edge of the Ile de la Cité, not far from the cathedral of Notre-Dame, stands the Royal Palace. It is made up of several buildings, constructed at different times, which rise in the midst of gardens and orchards. In the courtyard, Louis IX has recently built the Sainte-Chapelle. In a nearby building are the rooms where the Tresor de Chartres, the king's library and archives, are kept. At the moment the area around the palace is a huge building site. They are about to erect new buildings that will serve as the Curia regis, the Royal Court of Law and the Ministry of Finance.

Inside, the Royal Palace is breathtaking in its beauty. Where the old throne room used to be, you can admire the Great Hall made up of two enormous reception rooms on top of each other. On the ground floor, you will find the Great Lower Hall, also called the Gendarmes' Hall. This is over 230 feet long and is where the court personnel eat. On the top floor, you will find the vast and magnificent Great Upper Room. This is a huge space where you can see statues of all the French kings. It is reserved for important public ceremonies and for political meetings. The king wants no expense spared and has decided to have the walls of the Great Hall painted with scenes celebrating the glories of his dynasty,

The Louvre

At the end of the 12th century, Philip Augustus built a fortress that could not be taken by assault outside the new city walls. This is the Louvre. It is surrounded by four walls that have two gates, one leading to the Seine, the other to the city. The fortress is circled by a deep moat and is defended by ten towers, situated every 82 feet along the walls. At the center is a keep, a huge, round tower more than 100 feet high. The keep, or most secure part, is equipped to function as a royal residence, a prison, and even as the royal treasury. Louis IX has added a chapel and a Great Hall, or banquet room.

the Capetian Dynasty. The Royal Palace is surrounded by walls with two gates, one opens onto the Rue de la Barillerie and the other onto the Seine. The gate that opens onto the Seine has the Silver Tower on one side and Caesar's Tower on the other. How small the old buildings seem!

Go to the farthest point of the island and look over the Seine River. You will see the royal gardens where the kings usually receive the people of Paris on great occasions or to resolve legal disputes.

The Hotel-Dieu

Between the cathedral of Notre-Dame and the Seine River stands a large building called the Hotel-Dieu, which means the hostel or hotel of God. This is the oldest hospital in Paris. People say it was built by Bishop Landry in A.D. 651. In 1100, it was demolished to make way for the cathedral, then reconstructed at the edge of the churchyard. The new building was completed around 1260. The poor and the sick are accepted here, all except lepers, the crippled, those with incurable diseases, and the blind. The most serious cases are treated in the infirmary. Less serious cases are taken into the Saint-Denis room. The least serious cases,

together with those who are recovering are treated in the Saint-Thomas room. More recently, Louis IX has built the new room just for women. The clothes belonging to the sick are washed, mended, and kept in a place called the delousing room. In the wards, the sick lie nude, two, four, and at times even six to a bed. Often there are 1,000 sick people for the 300 beds. The floor is made of stone slabs. Each day, the sheets are changed and washed in the river. A servant has the special job of running after and bringing back the sheets that blow away from the washerwomen! The druggists prepare the medicines in the pharmacy using medicinal herbs grown in the hospital's vegetable garden. Surgical operations are performed by one of Paris's barbers. There are over one hundred of them

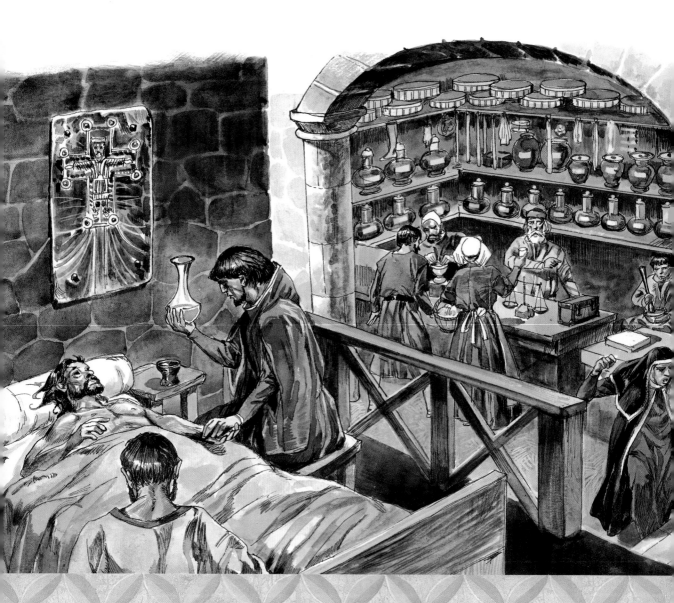

working in the city. Children run through the wards. They are the foundlings of Notre-Dame, who are brought up in the Hotel-Dieu. The hospital runs on alms and donations together with money raised from the sale of the produce grown on its land, the wine produced in its vineyards, and the animals bred in its stables. Unfortunately, many of the patients die and are buried in Saint-Innocent's cemetery. Other patients are discharged and regain their strength, in the open air, under the charming Parisian sky!

MEDICINE, ASTROLOGY, AND SUPERSTITION

People believe that Saints Cosmas and Damien protect doctors, chemists, and barbers, but they turn to astrology to protect themselves against illness. They believe that astrology influences their health. For example, they believe that the sun influences the right-hand side of the body together with their hearts, and the moon, the left-hand side together with their stomachs.

Life by the River

If you go to the Seine River for a swim, you may find yourself at the port of Gréve, which means gravel bed, on the right bank of the river. A great many boats tie-up at the quayside where crowds of workers are ready to transfer the goods from the ships onto carts or into the warehouses! The Seine is the chief communication route with Paris. It is easier, faster, and safer than the roads. Together with its tributaries—the Marne, the Oise, and the Yonne, the Seine provides a network of deep, wide waterways that have contributed to the commercial development of the city. Supplies of grains, wine, wood, salt, hay, animals for slaughter, and fish, together with different products from the fairs in the Champagne region, arrive at the port, and the products made by the Parisian craftsmen are taken away.

Some boats with only one boatman on board, a wine docker, go downstream in a line, tied together with ropes. Near the bridges, the waters of the Seine turn the many waterwheels to grind the corn that has just been unloaded. In the square facing onto the port is a labor market that has developed over the years. Here, the Parisian workers in search of work gather. The port of Greve is not the only one in Paris. If you go downstream, you will find the port of Ecole, which means intermediate port of call, near the church of Saint-Germain-l'Auxerrois. Then, on the northeast bank of the Ile de la Cité, the ports of Saint-Landry and Notre-Dame have developed. In order to really appreciate the fervor of life on the river why not let a ferryman take you from one side to the other?

THE WATER MERCHANTS

The water merchants have joined together to form a powerful guild of Seine boatmen. They supervise all the activities connected with the river. No boat, either loaded or empty, can navigate the river without their permission. All foreign vessels must have an agreement with a member of the Seine Boatmen's Guild. They supervise navigation and all the port operations. They hold the monopoly regarding the transport of certain goods and over the employment of the dockers. They are managed by one of Louis IX's civil servants, the prévot, or provost. The king has named him chief of all the merchants in the city. In this way the king has created a kind of City Council. The City Council meetings are held at the Parloir aux Bourgeois, near the Grand-Chatelet, which has become a kind of city hall. This is how the coat-of-arms of the boatmen has become the coat-of-arms of the city of Paris.

The Marais

If you look out toward the north from the city walls built by Philip Augustus, beyond the Saint-Martin gate, you will see a stretch of cultivated fields and a few ponds surrounded by gentle hills. This region is called the Marais, which means marshes. Once, this area was frequently flooded by the Seine. Now, it is no longer marshland. You can see farmers and peasants plowing and animals grazing in the fields along the gentle slopes of the Marais. The few marshy areas remaining near the river are home to ducks. Until the last century, the Marais was a vast,

uninhabited moor. You could only find a few churches, old abbeys, and tiny hamlets scattered around the countryside and on the hillsides. Since 1147, there has been a village for lepers here, the leper house of Saint-Lazare. The lepers are not allowed to enter the city of Paris.

Most of the Marais region belongs to religious orders. It was actually several monks, who began to reclaim and improve the land in 1154. They built numerous ditches. Water from the overflowing Seine was carried along the ditches to cultivate vegetables, grains, and vineyards. Today you can see vast estates, surrounded by dry stone walls. They are intensively cultivated and planted with fruit trees. These large farms belong not only to the religious orders, but also to the nobles and rich merchants who live inside the walls of Paris. The largest estate of all, the Cour-

tille Barbette, has given its name to the Barbette gate, one of the entrances to the city. Beside the important farms in the Grange-Bateliere, there are also smaller properties, like the one belonging to the Mathurins monks or the Petit-Marais del-Hotel-Dieu, which belongs to the hospital.

Along the paths crossing the Marais, it is not unusual to meet armed knights riding on the same horse. They are Knights Templar heading toward a castle, the one with the huge keep. This is the fortified monastery of the Temple. It is the headquarters of the richest, most powerful order of monks in France. It even keeps the king's treasure inside its walls. Those shabbily dressed knights, riding in pairs on the same horse, are only observing the rules of their order. Those rules do not allow the Knights Templar to travel alone!

THE KEEPERS OF THE ROYAL TREASURE.
Before leaving for the Crusades, Philip Augustus wrote a will stating that the royal treasure should be guarded in the keep of the Temple monastery where it could be safely protected by the strong, solid walls. Here the coffers, or strong boxes, and safes holding the revenues from the king's lands are also kept. Each coffer is locked with two keys. One is trusted to the Templars and the other to six representatives of the Parisian bourgeoisie, or middle classes.

The Halles

If you want to wander among market stalls, go and visit the Halles, the most important market in Paris. You will find it on the right bank of the Seine River, near the Saint-Innocent's cemetery. It rose from the old area called the Champeaux, or small fields. This region was reclaimed from the marshes and bought from King Louis VI, in 1135, to shelter the grain merchants, who came from the areas surrounding Paris. In 1141, the shopkeepers from Greve Square moved here. Afterward, Philip Augustus had walls with open galleries constructed to protect the market. He also had two covered buildings built to protect the wool merchants and weavers from thieves and from bad weather. In 1181, even the Saint-Ladre fair, which

had been held in the leper house of the same name, moved to the Halles. Later, Louis IX constructed other emporiums, or trade centers. These were for selling fish or to shelter peddlers. They were grouped in streets which took their names from the type of goods on sale. The market is open on Wednesdays, Fridays, and Saturdays. The king has the right to rent out the stalls and to charge a sales tax. As you can see, the Halles, also called the King's Market, is an enormous, colorful bazaar where everything is sold: woolen sheets, combs, wine, berets, bread, vegetables, eggs, sweets, and so much more. But no live animals are sold here. Animals are butchered in the quarter called the Boucherie (butcher's) near the Seine, to allow the butchers to use the river water. However, there is a fountain in the Halles. This draws water from a spring that

flows outside the city walls. Perhaps it is the same one the Parisians call the lovers' well. According to legend, here a young girl, betrayed in love, drowned herself long ago, and the well has since become the destination for lovers' pilgrimages.

The Pillory of the Halles

At the center of one of the crossroads in the Halles, you will find a strange construction in the middle of which is a rotating wheel. It is the king's pillory. Here merchants who are guilty of fraud or swearing are exposed to the public, their heads and hands locked in a wooden plank. They are punished like this for two hours a day for three consecutive markets. As the wheel turns, they are forced to suffer the insults of the public. They must put up with the rotten vegetables and mud people throw.

The Craftsmen

On the right bank of the Seine, near the Halles and the river port, the winding alleys are full of craftsmen's workshops. Here you will find an atmosphere of feverish activity. The alleys are crowded with people and traffic. Shopkeepers, merchants, customers, and apprentices rush around. You will see carts carrying bales of wool, bundles of skins, sacks of grain, barrels of wine, stones, and wood crisscrossing the street! There are over 5,000 craftsmen in Paris, working in over 300 different professions. A huge number work in textiles or as dyers. While a relatively few rich craftsmen own large shops and workshops, those belonging to most of the Parisian craftsmen are small. Almost all the

weavers live on the Rue de la Vielle Draperie, Old Drapery Street. Here they produce materials and cloths that will be transformed into elegant clothes or valuable decorations. Silk production is reserved for the women. They, too, have formed a guild of skilled craftswomen. But what is that terrible stink? It's coming from the workshops of the leather goods dealers' on the Rue des Pelletiers. Leather craftsmen boil up cauldrons of vegetable extracts and other weird ingredients to tan the skins that will shield the Parisians from the cold winters.

If you would like to see one of the activities that has made Paris famous, walk across to the left bank of the river. There, near the university, you will find the booksellers. Look at all those small workshops facing the street. That is where the parchment makers work. They make fine sheets of parchment paper from sheepskins. In one corner of the room, a few students copy texts for their professors. In smaller rooms, expert miniaturists and illuminators illustrate expensive volumes with beautiful scenes and elegant decorations. These books are intended for members of the nobility and for high-ranking Church officials. Paris is also a famous center for goldsmiths. Especially well known are the splendid boxes to hold holy relics, and chalices for the churches, the jewels of the royal treasury, gold and silver necklaces, small boxes inlaid with precious stones and enamel, and ivory ornaments. Clients

All the craftsmen who practice the same trade join a guild in order to be protected against any competition. So, they have elected a magistrate, the merchants' provost. One of the most famous provosts in Paris is Etienne Boileau, who, in 1268, decided to create the Book of the Trades. Here he wrote the statutes and rules of the trades in Paris. He accurately describes the hundreds of professions practiced in the city, the number of workshops, and the different techniques of production, together with the rules regulating the sales of each product.

throughout Europe buy the products of the Parisian craftsmen.

All of these small workshops are also retail shops and, sometimes, even dwellings. As you saunter around Paris you will also realize that many of these expert craftsmen are at work on the numerous building sites open in the capital. There are masons, carpenters, stonemasons, sculptors, painters, joiners, and glassmakers. The city is going through a period of transformation thanks to the construction of important works like the cathedral of Notre-Dame, the Sainte-Chapelle, the new university colleges, the King's Palace, and the many noblemen's homes being built within the city walls.

Apprentices, Workers, and Masters

Before you earn the qualification of craftsman and the right to open your own business, you have to work for several years for someone else. You begin as an apprentice to the master of a workshop. This is not an easy life. The apprentices live in the master's house. They pay him quite a big fee for their board, lodging, and for teaching them his craft. Apprentices are required to obey the master totally, and they cannot quit. At the end of a long and often difficult apprenticeship, the apprentice's status as manservant, or worker, is recognized by the master craftsman and confirmed by the members of the guild. Only then is the worker free to exercise his profession, by signing a contract for a fixed period with other master craftsmen.

You only become a real and fully accepted craftsman when you open your own workshop. Although some do become rich, the vast majority of craftsmen earn just enough to live on.

The Sainte-Chapelle

The whole of Paris is talking about the chasse (urn) that Louis IX has had built in the Royal Palace to house the relics of the Passion of Jesus. If you wish to visit, you will be escorted by a clergyman across a narrow courtyard, and you will discover not an urn but a chapel! You will marvel at this beautiful building. Its narrow, upward-thrusting lines, and high, stained-glass windows make it a real jewel of Gothic architecture. Its spires point elegantly toward the sky and are ringed with a crown of thorns made of stone. The chapel has two levels. The ground floor is reserved for the servants and the upper floor for the king and his family. The lower chapel looks rather like a crypt. The central nave is low. Short blue and red columns, decorated with the French lily and with golden towers, support the cross vaults high above. You climb up a spiral staircase to reach the upper chapel. There you will find yourself in a magic place full of light and glass. From the single nave rise pillars that support the splendid stained-glass windows, decorated with scenes from the

Bible and the Passion of Jesus. The vaulted ceiling is painted like a starry sky. The sun's rays flood the chapel, and violet reflected light gives the chapel an atmosphere of warm spirituality. You will see statues of the twelve apostles leaning against the pillars. Each golden capital has a different decoration. Look for the floral patterns including vine, oak, ivy, and holly leaves, also rose buttercup and violet patterns. If you look really carefully, you will even make out the shape of a lizard or a bird. The relics are kept behind the altar, in the platform under the canopy. All

the relics are believed to be from Jesus' Cru-
cifiction. Just imagine, this jewel of a chapel
was built in only five or six years, perhaps by
the architect of Notre-Dame.
Louis IX did not want to be sep-
arated from the precious
relics bought from the
emperor of Constantino-
ple. The chapel, conse-
crated in 1248, cost a great
deal, too—40,000 "torneses"
or ancient coins!

**The Art of Creating
Stained-Glass Windows**

Master stained-glass makers created
the windows in the Sainte-Chapelle. To
achieve this, they fused sand with finely
ground precious stones. On a wooden
table, they drew the design using the
actual size they would need in the window.
Once the glass was cut, they painted the
different scenes or designs needed to com-
plete the picture. Then each was fitted into
a netlike, lead framework to ensure its
resistance to wind and bad weather.

Life in a Monastery

As you wander through the city, you may come across an imposing group of religious buildings, including a large church and various other buildings, together with vegetable gardens, orchards, fields, and vineyards. This is one of the many abbeys in Paris. Like you, many people approach the entrance door. They may be travelers, pilgrims, or poor, sick people looking for shelter. The monks are extremely hospitable. They take in whoever needs refuge for the night and provide a bowl of hot soup as well. Join the line! It is a good opportunity to visit the abbey. The Guardian Friar will lead you through well-kept vegetable gardens and orchards where the monks grow fruits, vegetables, and medicinal herbs. Then he will take you to guestrooms, in a building set slightly apart from the rest of the abbey. Here the guests are refreshed and fed. The life in the abbey revolves around the church and the cloister. The rooms where the monks dedicate themselves to their various occupations face the cloister.

The abbot is the head of the community. He is responsible for the religious services and manages the offerings, donations, and church money. He is actively involved in relations with the outside world, helping the poor and the sick. He also makes sure that the rules of his order are strictly followed. Monks who come from noble families spend a large part of their time in the scriptorium, dedicated to teaching, studying the Sacred Scriptures, and copying precious manuscripts. The monastery libraries are therefore rich in rare and valuable volumes. The poorer friars, most of whom cannot read or write, are usually given the more humble tasks. They have to work in the laundry, in the dormitories, in the fields, in the kitchens, and perform all the most tiring jobs. A monk's

day is above all reserved for prayer. At fixed hours of the day and night, they interrupt whatever they are doing to speak to God. Even during their frugal meals, eaten in the refectory, they meditate on passages from the Sacred Scriptures read aloud by a fellow monk. Little time is left for leisure.

Abbeys and Religious Orders in Paris.

The oldest abbeys in Paris are the abbeys of Sainte-Genevieve, Saint-Germain-des-Prés, Saint-Martin-des-Champs, and Saint-Victor. Almost all belong to the Cluniac or Cistercian orders, which developed in France inspired by the Order of Saint Benedict. Among the other congregations there are the Monks of the Trinity, who dedicate themselves to ransoming Christians taken prisoner by the infidels, and the Servants of Mary, who are called the White Cloaks because of what they wear.

29

The Victory at Bouvines

If you had been in Paris on a summer day in 1214, you would have seen a great celebration. Let us look back on that glorious day. It is sunset. King Philip Augustus (Phillip II) is returning to Paris after his victory over the enemies of France at Bouvines, in the region of Flanders. King Philip and the forces of France fought a fierce battle against Emperor Otto IV, John Lackland, king of England, and their allies the feudal lords. When the royal procession, announced by horns and drums, approaches the city walls, a huge crowd of citizens bursts through the Saint-Jacques gate to welcome the victors. You can see the king, followed by his infantry and his brave knights. Behind them come their prisoners, bedraggled and wounded, still wearing their armor. As a sign of scorn, the prisoners have been piled onto a cart of smelly, vile stuff, and now they have to endure the insults of the young people as they pass. Following the prisoners come the carts carrying the spoils of war. They are loaded with coffers full of money and jewels; bales of cloth and precious tapestries from Flanders; weapons, supplies, and other goods. After a hard day's work in the fields, the peasants run to join in

the celebrations, scattering flowers and leafy branches along the street. The youngest Parisians dance and sing. The procession enters the city at dusk, lit by thousands of torches, while all the church bells of Paris ring out in celebration.

Colorful drapes and banners hang from the windows of the houses. A procession of university professors and students comes down from the Sainte-Genevieve Abbey to meet their monarch. Another procession comes from the Rue Saint-Denis, headed by members of the clergy and the trade associations. Together, they will all go to the chapel of the Royal Palace to thank God and to return the Oriflamme banner.

What Is the Oriflamme?
The oriflamme is a three-cornered red banner, fringed with green and gold. It used to be the flag of the abbot of Saint-Denis, but now it has become the symbol of royal power. It follows the king during battle.

The City Walls Built by Philip Augustus

During the 12th century, Paris grew enormously. So, in 1190, King Philip Augustus began to construct a large circle of walls that surround not only the city, but the ancient abbey of Sainte-Genevieve together with part of the Marais region as well. These new walls are around 39 feet high and at least 10 feet wide. They circle the city for more than 3 miles. On the ramparts, there are walkways protected by wooden parapets and solid stone walls. Along the walls you will find 70 defense towers and 16 gates with iron gratings at a gateway. These can be lowered to prevent passage.

The University

If you go a little farther into the neighborhoods on the left bank of the Seine River, you will meet a number of clerics and several young men with shaven heads. The clerics are teachers or professors; and the others are students. Many schools exist in this part of the city, belonging to the many monasteries in the area. The student clerics, or clergy, have shaven heads. Or they wear the tonsure, which is the official term for the circle shaved on the crown of their heads, because they wish to follow a career in the Church. Teaching is the special right of the Church, so most of the teachers are priests. These schools attract students from all over Europe.

They are very famous because great masters like Thomas Aquinas, Bonaventure, and the poet Rutebeuf teach here. Nowadays the teaching is done in abbeys and convents, but until quite recently, students followed the lessons in workshops, granaries, or stables, often seated on piles of hay. The Rue du Fouarre earned its name this way, as did Hay Street, where the Faculty of the Arts has its headquarters. The growing number of students has given rise to the recent creation of a free association called the University, which enjoys considerable freedom. Rich students pay for their lessons, food, and lodgings. Poor students work as book copyists or even as servants to pay for theirs. To help the most needy students, religious orders and private citizens have set up a system of student grants.

The College of Theology, founded in 1257 by Robert de Sorbon, is particularly famous. The University is developing around this. But whatever is all that noise ahead? This is just the students, enjoying sports' activities and team games in a space reserved for them called the Pré-aux-clercs, which literally means "the lawn for those wearing the tonsure." Some of the students are fighting furiously! Really, they should be behaving meekly and showing devotion to religious principles. But they are young, and they enjoy having fun, singing, and playing jokes on one another. Who knows how they will celebrate getting their diplomas!

The University Courses

The University of Paris is divided into four faculties: Arts, Canon (or church) Law, Medicine, and Theology. The Faculty of Arts is the most popular. You can begin studying here at the age of 14. You will learn one of 2 courses of study. One includes grammar, rhetoric, and logic. The other includes arithmetic, geometry, music, and astronomy. After receiving a diploma in the Arts, at the age of 20, a student can choose between the Faculty of Medicine, Law, or Theology. The first takes 5 or 6 years, but theology demands 15 years of study.

STUDENT PUNISHMENTS

Students who do not respect the rules or who commit serious pranks are not physically punished, but they do have to pay heavy fines. Pupils from the Sorbon College who stay out all night have to pay a fine amounting to two and a half pennies; which is a lot! But there are colleges that fine their students even more heavily. For example, if a student from Harcourt College gets drunk at a tavern, he has to pay a fine of six pennies.

The Theater

In the streets of Paris you may come across a town-crier announcing in a loud voice a theatrical performance at Notre-Dame. This is a very popular event and attracts a large audience. The stage is built on the cathedral steps and in the church square. The facade of the cathedral behind the stage makes an ideal backdrop for the performance. Three scenes are set on the stage. They represent Earth, Heaven, and Hell. At the far side of one-half of the stage, the producer presents Hell like the mouth and throat of a dragon, spitting out black-painted devils. In the center of the stage, Earth is symbolized by a chair, which suggests a palace belonging to a king or bishop. Or perhaps a table, jugs, and a candle are in the center of the stage to give the idea of a tavern. There may even be an iron grill, to suggest a prison. At the edge of the other side of the stage, a throne surrounded by saints and angels symbolizes Heaven. On other occasions, there is a tomb and a cross representing the Passion of Christ. The religious story that is performed changes according to what feast is being celebrated. It may be Christmas, Easter, a saint's day, or a feast honoring a miracle.

All the actors are men. The youngest men play the women's parts. Although Latin is the language of the Church, the theatrical performances given on the cathedral steps and in the church square are given in French. Improvisation is common, and the text is often interrupted by sung passages and by dances.

The theater is a great collective event. The audience enjoys taking part, noisily showing their emotions, their wonder, approval, or fear. Sometimes the performances last several days. During the intermissions, the audience is entertained by jugglers and fire-eaters, or by the songs and verses of minstrels.

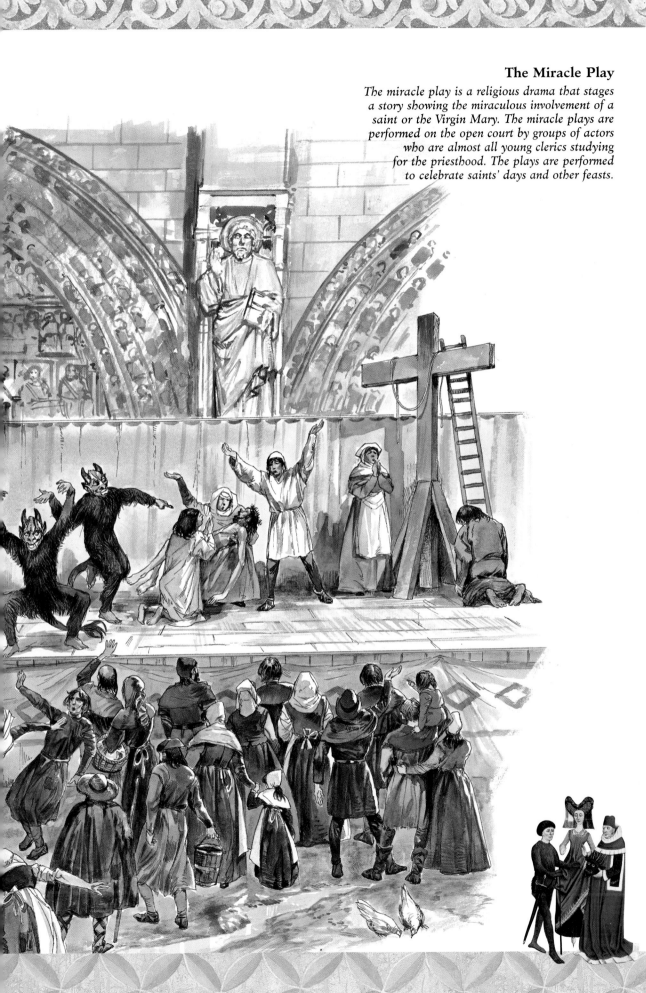

The Miracle Play

The miracle play is a religious drama that stages a story showing the miraculous involvement of a saint or the Virgin Mary. The miracle plays are performed on the open court by groups of actors who are almost all young clerics studying for the priesthood. The plays are performed to celebrate saints' days and other feasts.

The Banquet

If a nobleman invites you to a banquet, prepare yourself for a feast! The guests sit in the brightly lit Great Hall around beautifully set tables. The host sits in the center at a table on a raised platform. His most important guests and the women of highest rank present sit beside him. At the sound of a horn, servants enter, bringing silver bowls full of water perfumed with rose petals, for the guests to wash their hands. Then the courses are brought, one after another. The menu begins with fruit of the season and different salads. Then follow soups and consommes, served in bowls, one shared between every two diners. After this, the main dish of various types of roast meat is served. Quarters of beef and veal, legs of mutton, goat, and lamb are brought to the tables. They are served with spicy sauces or seasoned with herbs and spices that have pleasing aromas. Game, hunted on the nobleman's lands is also served. Except for the soup, guests eat with their hands. From the serving board, the food is placed by the guests themselves onto a large slice of bread, that they use as a plate. Wine is poured into crystal goblets, or goblets made of gold or silver. There is a pause between courses when the diners are entertained by the singing of minstrels, accompa-

nied by the lute and drums, and by acrobats and jugglers. The ladies present may sing and dance together in a round dance between courses while the men chat and drink.

Other delicious dishes follow, like pheasant pie, decorated with the beautiful feathers of the male pheasant, or poultry covered with honey and goldleaf. Then comes dessert—sweet rolls and delicate wafers. The final course includes sweetmeats, candied fruit, and cheeses, with a special wine to which honey has been added. All that is really enough to fill you up! But there is more. Delicious sweets and candies made from ginger are served to help you digest the meal you have just eaten. What an unforgettable banquet!

Table Manners

At the table, be careful not to lick your fingers! Instead, clean them on the tablecloth or with the napkins brought by the servants. Before drinking, you should wipe your mouth.

Avoid making a slurping noise when drinking. Also, do not gulp your drink. Finally, lower-ranking guests should never drink a toast before those from a higher social level.

Streets and Houses

Almost all the streets of Paris are made of packed earth. A gutter runs down the middle of each street to drain off liquids. When you walk through Paris, you will find the streets full of bustle and activity. You will meet housewives hurrying to do their shopping, children chasing each other, shouting at the tops of their voices, peasants with carts drawn by oxen, carrying their vegetables to be sold at the market, shepherds leading their flocks to be slaughtered at the butcher's. Everywhere you will see the poor, the old, the crippled, and the beggars, all in search of food, alms, and charity. Along the streets, the craftsmen work out in the open, in front of their shops. Each shop has a window with a folding shutter, which can also be used as a stall to display their goods. The landlords

stand at the doors of their taverns calling out the merits of their food and wine to the travelers who pass by. The houses are grouped into blocks. They are narrow, made of wood, mud, and straw and are between two and four stories high. At the back there is almost always a yard or a vegetable garden.

The floors are made of packed earth that is sometimes covered with wooden planks. Fresh leafy branches are spread over the

floors to keep them clean. Few windows have glass. People protect themselves from the cold with sheets of parchment or oilcloth, that allow a dim light to seep through into the rooms. Wood and straw are piled under the roof in the attic, and fires often break out, destroying whole blocks of houses. The houses are simply furnished. Poor families live crowded into a single room, with a fireplace for cooking and a straw mattress to sleep on. Merchants and craftsmen have more comfortable houses. Their kitchens are large and heated. Meat is hung under the chimney cover to smoke. There is not much furniture—a table, a few benches, a chest to store linens, and one bed for the whole family.

THE CEMETERY OF THE INNOCENTS
Beside each religious building in Paris is a piece of land where all the people from the neighborhood are buried. The rich and important people enjoy the privilege of being buried inside the churches. The largest cemetery is the Cemetery of the Innocents, near the Halles. People neither fear nor respect this sacred place. Children play among the tombs, and shopkeepers from the nearby markets come here to sell their goods. At night, tramps and animals wander undisturbed among groups of gamblers and people having fun dancing, singing, and merrymaking! For this reason, the king has had a high wall built around the Cemetery of the Innocents. He has also issued severe orders to keep people away from cemeteries in general, not just out of respect for the dead, but for health reasons.

The Pilgrimage to Mont-Saint-Michel

If you are in Paris in September, you may want to visit the abbey on Mont-Saint-Michel on September 29, the feast of Saint-Michael. Over 10,000 pilgrims visit there each year. The sanctuary stands on the shores of the Atlantic Ocean. You travel by horse or mule along one of the official routes, called the routes to paradise. The journey is not an easy one and takes several weeks. Along the way you will come across many pilgrims traveling on foot, some alone, but many in groups to better defend themselves from bandits and thieves. They all hope that the Marvel, as Mont-Saint-Michel is called, will soon come into view. Pilgrims wear capes with hoods and wide-brimmed hats, and they carry haversacks, or backpacks. They also carry staffs, the typical stick used by travelers to lean on as they walk. Follow the pilgrims if you wish to find food and lodging in the monasteries, churches, or lodgings along the route. As you approach the abbey, notice its imposing walls and high windows. Before venturing onto the narrow causeway of earth and sand that separates the abbey from the mainland, check the surrounding water. At high tide Mont-Saint-Michel becomes an island! Look out for the quicksand, too.

Once you go through the main gate, clamber up the steep path as far as the chaplain's house, where the pilgrims are welcomed and given refreshment. The more important people are given hospitality on the upper floor. Higher still, the building develops on three levels, where you will find the refectory and the beautiful cloister, which invites you to meditation and prayer. The view from the top is magnificent, and from there you begin to appreciate how much effort must have been required to construct the church here. Pilgrims also come from far and wide to obtain precious relics. So, when you leave do not forget to take a few relics with you; such as a lead medallion, a shell, or a vial of holy water. You might even take a little sand from the bay.

The Legend of Mont-Saint-Michel

Near Mont-Saint-Michel there was once a forest that was covered by the sea, leaving only a large cliff called Mount Tomb above the level of the water. In 708, Bishop Aubert di Avranches dreamed that the Archangel Michael asked him to erect a sanctuary on its summit. The legend says that Bishop Aubert also struck a rock with his pastoral staff from which sprang a miraculous fountain with the power to cure various diseases. Several miracles have led to Mont-Saint-Michel's fame, and it quickly became a popular destination for pilgrims.

The Lendit Fair

In Paris, at the beginning of the summer, near the famous Saint-Denis Abbey, the oldest fair in France is held. This is the Lendit fair, which has been famous since the 7th century, when it was a honey market. The bishop himself leads a solemn procession from the cathedral of Notre-Dame to Saint-Denis where he opens the fair and blesses all the merchants. There are neat rows of stalls and tents. Merchants who come from the same area are grouped together in "streets." So you can find Lisieux Street, Vire Street, and Bernay Street, for example, together with merchants from the four streets in Rouen called the Halles. Here the shopkeepers from that city display their cloth. The stalls are identified with painted signs, like shops. You can find a huge variety of products ranging from the cheapest to the most expensive: foods, skins, animals, furnishings, weapons, objects worked in gold, and parchment. Numerous moneychangers convert foreign money, or money from other French cities, into Parisian money. Occasionally a messenger on horseback arrives to give the merchants

letters containing detailed instructions about prices and information regarding the sales of their goods. Special magistrates go around the fair. It is their job to check the weights and measures being used, together with the quality of the goods on sale. They also have to make sure that frauds or thefts are not committed. An enormous crowd throngs through the market, some out of curiosity, others ready to buy. Some just look, others touch, try on, taste, bargain, deal, buy, quarrel, and generally have fun. They watch the jugglers improvising street performances to show off their skills and look on in amusement as children and old folk watch, spellbound.

THE FAIRS OF THE CHAMPAGNE REGION

The Lendit fair is not the most famous fair in France. Those of the Champagne and Brie regions are much more well known. Their geographical position, along the route between Flanders and Italy, attracts merchants from many countries. These fairs are held in different cities during the course of the year. The first, in January, is in Lagny. Then, in the middle of Lent, a fair is held in Bar-sur-Aube. The Provins fair follows in May, and in June, the Troyes fair, nicknamed "the hot fair." In September, a second fair is held in Provins, and the season ends with the "cold fair" in Troyes.

Hunting in Fontainebleau

If you want to take part in a hunting expedition in the forest of Fontainebleau, which is about 60 kilometers from Paris, you will need to find a good horse. After a long gallop through a wooded region dotted with villages and cultivated fields, you will reach a huge forest. Before entering the dense tangle of trees and branches you need to remember that the forest is full of dangerous animals, including many wolves! Take care that the gamekeeper does not mistake you for a poacher. In fact, the forest belongs to various lords and above all to the king of France, who is the only person who can exercise the right to hunt there. The furious barking of the dogs, straining on leashes held by the beaters, announces the arrival of the monarch and his retinue on the tracks of a wild boar. A little way off, a noblewoman is

THE NAME OF THE FOREST
The name Fontainebleau seems to come from the name of an ancient lord of the region called Blaudus or Blealdus, or from a fountain that had especially clear, blue water. But there is a legend, too, which recalls a greyhound named Bleau. This dog used to hunt with Louis IX, and the king was very fond of him. The legend says that this dog discovered a spring in the forest.

hunting with a falcon. The falcon is trained to swoop down onto other birds in flight or onto smaller prey found on the ground. As you can see, hunting is one of the favorite pastimes of the aristocracy. At the end of the day, the king and his courtiers leave the rich spoils of the hunt, including deer, wild boar, hare, roebuck, pheasant, and other game animals with the servants. Back at the castle a sumptuous banquet will be prepared. While in the forest, you will certainly have come across peasants, intent on gathering fruit, acorns, mushrooms, herbs, firewood, and honey, or pasturing their sheep in the clearings. The boldest defy the royal laws against public hunting and go poaching. For them, hunting is not a pastime, it is a way to avoid starving!

Crusaders and Foot Soldiers

What large numbers of armed men you see in Paris! But these men are not members of an army, all wearing the same uniform. From the different emblems on their tunics you can recognize the soldiers of the company of guards serving in the city. Paris is the headquarters of the royal court, so you will see many knights riding through the streets. This is the most select corps of the king's army. Astride his trusty steed, the knight rides into battle armed with his sword and lance, protected by a long hauberk, a coat of iron chain-mail that covers his legs, and by a helmet. The nobles have many men in their retinue who wear their banner, a sign made of a square piece of cloth with the nobleman's coat of arms painted on it. The knights are escorted by mounted sergeants who are neither noble nor rich, and who cannot afford expensive weapons or armor. They wear sleeveless chain mail coats or leather tunics, and small, cone-shaped helmets to protect their heads. The foot soldiers are not real soldiers. They are peasants who leave their farms to fight for the king. They wear leather tunics and are armed with bows, swords, axes, clubs, and long, hooked pikes used for unsaddling enemy knights. In battle their lines walk toward the enemy. They cover for the crossbowmen and the knights, the higher ranks who decide the outcome of the battle.

The Municipal Guards

Two types of guet (guard), two police forces, serve the city of Paris—the royal guards and the guards of the guilds. Both forces are under the direction of the municipal council. Dozens of guards, on foot or on horseback, watch continuously over the city. They are under the command of a special knight of the watch. The night watch in the local neighborhoods is trusted to members of the voluntary service provided by the guilds. The citizens' guards patrol the streets and watch over the walls. They guarantee public order, hunt thieves and criminals, and make sure the municipal regulations regarding taxes and the sale of goods are respected.

The Rich, Gallant Crusaders

You will recognize the crusaders by the cross on their capes. Usually they are warrior monks, Knights Hospitallers, or Knights Templars, belonging to the orders of Saint John of Jerusalem or of the Temple. Both orders were begun in the 11th century, to help poor pilgrims on their way to the Holy Land. These congregations are organized along military lines. For example, the head of the Templars is the Grand Master assisted by the Grand Officers. Decisions are made by the assembly or chapter of the knights. The order has many centers, which are responsible for collecting money for the Crusades. In the Holy Land, the crusaders have won enough fiefs and riches to become the bankers of the king of France. Their treasures, arrogance, and show of luxury have made them unpopular with the ordinary people.

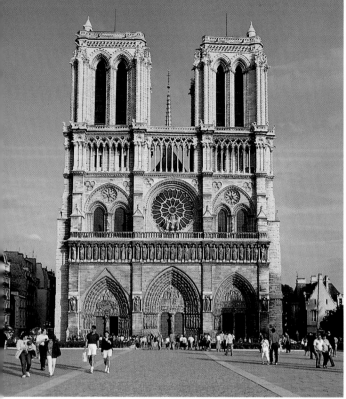

Present-Day Paris

Paris has been called the City of Lights. Seeing it at night confirms that statement without a doubt. Strolling up the Champs Elysées toward the Arc de Triomphe gives you a wonderful sense of the vitality of the city. Walking through the broad avenues, or the tiny streets of the Left Bank, will also tell the story of the many ages of this magnificent city and its glorious history.

You have so many sites to enjoy in Paris, you are going to find it hard to choose. At the Cluny Museum you can see the unicorn tapestries and the foundation of a Roman ruins at that same spot. The Louvre, with its glass pyramid entrance, houses many masterpieces. At the top of the grand staircase, you will be greeted by Nike of Samothrace. Also known as "Winged Victory," this statue is an unforgettable thrill. Don't miss the Venus de Milo. The foundation of the Louvre is on a special display, so that the earliest layers of this building can be studied here, too. You can also visit the City of Science and Industry and experience an interactive science museum.

The Luxembourg Gardens offer a place to sit and read, though you will not be allowed to walk on that lush green grass. Paris offers a special fascination for all who visit it. Few can come away without wonderful memories of the people, the food, and the splendor that is Paris.

Notre-Dame

After the Eiffel Tower, Notre-Dame, the Roman Catholic cathedral built on the Ile de la Cité, is one of the great symbols of Paris. Built in the Middle Ages in what was then the new Gothic style, it is a "must" for visitors to Paris today. The cathedral suffered damage and deterioration over the centuries and had to be restored in the 19th century. Only the three great rose windows have kept their 13th-century glass. When you visit this cathedral, leave time to climb up the 223-foot-high towers, for a very special view of the city and the Seine. Remember to take your camera!

You can stand in front of Notre-Dame in the afternoon sunshine and then walk along the Seine to see the flying buttresses around the eastern end of this great building. Or you can see it again in the evening with lights illuminating it.

Gargoyle

This is one of the many gargoyles that decorate the edge of the roof on the cathedral of Notre-Dame. Shaped like monsters and dragons, these gargoyles collect the rainwater from the roof gutters and channel it to spout away from the cathedral walls.

The Pont-Neuf

Although its name means "new bridge," the Pont-Neuf is the oldest of the Paris bridges. In fact, it was the first sidewalk of Paris. Street vendors set up shop here, and for 200 years, this bridge was the main street of the city. Begun in 1578, the bridge was completed in 1604. It was so well built and has lasted so long that Parisians often say something is "as solid as the Pont-Neuf." Such an old bridge needs regular repair, but as you walk over the Pont-Neuf in Paris today, you are walking on what is, for the most part, the original bridge.

The Place des Vosges

Located in the Marais, this is one of the most elegant residential squares in Paris. The Marais, no longer marshland outside the city walls, is now an essential part of Paris. Originally called Place Royal, the square has been called the Place des Vosges since 1800. The three-story houses shown here are made of red brick with white stone. The ground floors form the arcades you can walk through along the sidewalks.

The Halles

This is the modern group of architecture and gardens built between 1971 and 1979 in the area of Paris where the original central market of Paris, Les Halles, stood from 1183 to 1969. When the market was moved to a new location near Orly, the old market halls were used for cultural events and exhibitions. Then, in 1971, they were torn down and the building of a new complex, called the Forum des Halles, was begun. Here you will find the Pompidou National Center for Art and Culture. This houses the National Museum of Modern Art, the multimedia Public Information Library, the Industrial Design Center, and the Institute for Acoustic and Musical Research.

The Sainte-Chapelle

The Sainte-Chapelle, or "Holy Chapel," is one of the great monuments of France. Built under King Louis IX's direction in the 13th century, between 1243 and 1248, it can be found in the palace courtyards of the Palace of Justice on the Ile de la Cité. Sainte-Chapelle has vaulted ceilings on a framework of slender columns, and the walls in between are made of stained glass. The chapel was designed to hold the Crown of Thorns thought to be the actual one worn by Jesus.

Saint-Germain-des-Prés

Saint-Germain-des-Prés, the oldest church in Paris, no longer sits surrounded by fields and countryside. An urban area, called Saint-Germain-des-Prés, has been built up around the church. Today, the area is as famous for its narrow streets lined with antique shops, its cafes, and its nightlife, as for its lovely church. The present church contains a mixture of elements from different ages: the 6th century marble columns; the 12th century chancel, sheltered walkway of the original cloister, and bell tower; and the 17th century vaulted ceiling in the nave. The area contains several museums, the Sorbonne (University of Paris), art galleries, and bookshops. Its special atmosphere makes it popular with a great many people, both young and old.

Mont-Saint-Michel

One of the most popular tourist venues in France, Mont-Saint-Michel stands on a rocky islet off the coast of Normandy in the English Channel. The mount, or rock, is surrounded by vast sand banks and only becomes an island when tides are particularly high. An ancient abbey sits atop the mount. If you plan to visit the abbey, get ready for a steep climb! And don't forget to visit the crypts. Looking down over the abbey's medieval walls, you can enjoy a wonderful view of the bay. From the abbey you can also look down on the village below. Some of the houses along the narrow streets winding up to the abbey date back to the 15th century.

Fontainebleau

The chateau of Fontainebleau is one of the most impressive residences built by the kings of France. Originally a medieval royal hunting lodge, it was enlarged by Louis IX in the 13th century and was completely rebuilt in the 16th century. The vast gardens, lakes, and fountains you can see today, were redesigned during the reign of Louis XIV. In the winter of 1999/2000, a catastrophic storm uprooted hundreds of magnificent old trees from the scenic wooded areas in the famous forest of Fontainebleau. This forest extends over 42,000 acres near the chateau. A massive replantation program has begun to restore the forest of Fontainebleau.

Important Dates

Roman and Medieval Paris • Paris has been an important center since ancient times. In the 3rd century B.C., Celtic peoples called the Parisii were already established in the area. The city was named after them. At the approach of Caesar's Roman legions in 53 B.C., the inhabitants set fire to the city. Later it was rebuilt by the Romans and given the name Lutetia Parisorum. It was destroyed by the Barbarians and rebuilt in the 6th century by King Clovis, who made it the capital of his kingdom. In the centuries that followed, Paris was sacked several times by the Normans. A narrow circle of walls was raised for protection, which limited trade to exchanges within the immediate area around the city. After the year A.D. 1000, the city expanded greatly. This was due to the economic activity that developed along the Seine River, the fairs that were held periodically in the region, and the administrative functions concentrated around the bishop's seat and the Royal Palace.

Philip Augustus • In the 13th century, Philip Augustus unified France by his victory, at the battle of Bouvines in 1214, over the great vassals and the king of England, who still owned a large number of territories in France. At the same time, Philip set about strengthening the state's authority, which was continually threatened by the powers of the local lords. He did this by establishing new ways of administering finance and justice.

The Age of Louis IX • The work of Philip Augustus was completed by his nephew Louis IX, who was crowned king when he was only 12 years old. Louis IX, who later became Saint Louis, was a religious man and embodied the idea of a knightly king. He was a lover of peace. But as an energetic defender of the faith, he proclaimed two crusades to free the Holy Land, in 1248 and 1270. The enterprise failed, and during the second holy war, Louis IX died in Tunis. Although his crusades were not successful, Louis IX was successful politically at home. He reestablished the authority of the state throughout France by instituting a corps of royal civil servants to administer justice fairly and swiftly.

France enjoyed great prosperity during his reign. The cities flourished. The countryside underwent great development due to the cultivation of vines and grains. Paris, situated at the center of a rich, densely populated region, became the first city in a European state to become a real capital city. It was a hub of international traffic, prosperous crafts industries, and because of its university, was at the crossroads of culture, the arts, and the sciences.

The Reign of Philip IV, the Fair • In 1285, Philip IV, son of Philip III, the Bold, came to the throne of France. He continued the work to strengthen royal power begun by his predecessors. During this time, a long period of conflict with the papacy began. France needed money to finance the war with Flanders. So the king decided to reduce the Church's immunity from taxation. Pope Boniface VIII was so offended by this measure that he excommunicated the king. Philip IV, supported by his subjects, invaded Italy with a military expedition that stormed and took the fortress at Anagni, where the pope had barricaded himself. This episode was extremely humiliating for the papacy and a triumph for the French monarchy.

Paris at the End of the 13th Century • At the end of the 13th century, Paris could be divided into three distinct zones, inside the walls built by Philip Augustus. In the center, was the island, which held the centers of temporal power, the king, the administration of justice and finance, and the municipal authorities, and the center of religious power, the bishop. On the right bank of the Seine River was the center of the industrious and commercial life of the city, with the Halles and the river port. Finally, on the left bank of the Seine were the schools and the monasteries, where students flocked to study, attracted by the reputation of one of the first European universities.

Glossary

arc-boutant, or flying-buttress In Gothic architecture an arch that looks like a goose's neck, because it has two ends which lean against the external walls of a building at different heights. Its function is to support the thrust of the vaults.

barber The barber shaves beards and cuts hair. But in Medieval times, he is also the dentist and the surgeon. When surgery is needed, he replaces the doctor, who does not perform operations. In 1292 there were as many as 151 barbers in Paris. They formed a guild and were often called to operate in the hospitals.

Chasse, or reliquary An urn or small box, which is usually shaped like a church. The relics of saints are kept inside. A chasse is normally made of gilded wood or glass, and is sometimes adorned with gems or carved decorations, or even painted.

chef-d'oeuvre The masterpiece that a craftsman must create at the end of his apprenticeship, according to the rules of art set down by his guild, in order to obtain the qualification of mastercraftsman.

cleric, or minor clerk A cleric who has received the tonsure but is still a student and has not yet entered the Church. In a general sense it refers to an educated person, as most of the cultured people in Parisian society at this time are members of religious orders and institutions.

crieur This word comes from the verb *crier*, which means to shout, and refers to the peddler who advertises his wares by shouting aloud in the streets. Hard-working crieurs repair clothes, renovate furniture, or announce that the public baths are ready. As they had become a recognized public service, the crieurs formed their own guild, which Philip Augustus merged with the powerful water-merchants' guild in 1220.

guet A guard or watchman, in particular, the night watchmen. There are two types of guard in Paris, the king's guard, which is the city police force, and the guilds' guards, appointed directly by the guilds. Both bodies are commanded by the knight of the guards, who is nominated by the king.

jeu, or play A theatrical work in verse, which may be sacred or profane in nature. This form of theater uses dialogue, songs, music, and dance and is based on dramatic or comic situations or ideas. Sometimes the performances last several days.

jongleur A kind of minstrel, who writes verses and sings songs, also a juggler who can perform clever tricks. You can see them in the squares, in the markets, and at fairs. Sometimes they are engaged by the nobles to entertain their guests at celebrations and banquets.

livre This word comes from the Latin word libra, or balance, and has several meanings. As a measure of weight, the livre is equal to about 360 grams. As a coin, its value varies depending on location. For example, the city of Tours has a Tornese livre that has a different value than the Parisian livre. La livre is not to be confused with *le livre,* which means "book."

métier This word means "job," "profession." But it also means "guild," the corporation or association of all those who work at a particular job, whether the work is manual or intellectual. The guild fixes extremely precise rules for doing specific jobs. It sets the materials that should be used, the prices that should be charged, and the hierarchy of work, that is, which level of worker should perform which job.

oublie A light, thin wafer, like the Communion Host. Its name comes from the Latin word oblata, or offering. Made from flour, water, wine, and sometimes eggs, it is a typical sweet eaten at celebrations. It is cooked between round, iron plates and then rolled up. The sweets are also sold by peddlers in the streets.

paté, or paste A dish made from dough that is filled with some kind of food before cooking it in an oven.

prevot This word means commissioner, a civil servant appointed to manage a guild.

Further Reading

Barron's Educational Editors. *Life in the Middle Ages.* (Megascope series). Barron, 1998.

Bussolin, Veronique. *France.* (Country Fact Files series). Raintree Steck-Vaughn, 1995.

Fisher, Teresa. *France.* (Food and Festivals series). Raintree Steck-Vaughn, 1999.

Holmes, Burton. *Paris.* (World 100 Years Ago series). Chelsea House, 1999.

Marshall, Chris. *Warfare in the Medieval World.* (History of Warfare series). Raintree Steck-Vaughn, 1998.

Ngcheong-Lum, Roseline. *France.* (Countries of the World series). Gareth Stevens, Inc., 1999.

Perdrizet, Marie-Pierre. *Cathedral Builders.* (Peoples of the Past series). Millbrook Press, 1992.

Rice, Earle, Jr. *Life During the Crusades.* (Way People Live series). Lucent Books, 1997.

Roland, Susan. *France, the Crossroads of Europe.* (Discovering Our Heritage series). Silver Burdett Press, 1998.

Stein, R. Conrad. *Paris.* (Cities of the World series). Childrens, 1996.

Wright, Nicola. *France and French.* Barron, 1993.

Index